Love my hair

Written by A M Colman

Illustrated by Russ Daff

Design by Mark Walling

for Leah, Mum & Nanny Jean

ISBN 978-1-99-96786-0-9 | © 2018 Angelbooks All rights reserved

Hi, my name is Leah and I really love my hair.
Even when it's in a tangle and looks like I don't care.

Lucy's hair is really long and looks kind of ginger.

Marcus has such tight tight curls,
you can wrap them around your finger.

Miriam's hair cannot be seen but I saw it at her house.

Phillip has a medical problem,
so his hair is as short as a mouse.

Adeola has her hair in plaits and changes it all the time.

Kim's hair is a bit like mine, but it is very fine.

Ali's hair grows really fast so he has it cut a lot.

Kevin's hair is really light. He avoids the sun in case it gets too hot.

Michael does not like his hair being done so sometimes it's a mess.

Kujaro loves his short hair and parting and says it looks the best.

I have learnt a lot about us and how different we all are. Every child should know they are special and that they are a star.

I don't have to look like you and it's ok you're not like me. My hair is mine and yours is yours and we are all as cool as can be.

Love my hair

Angelbooks aim to encourage children and adults to feel at home in their skin, their community and the world.

As you know books are like windows and Mirrors. We all need to be able to see a reflection of ourselves wherever we are, and we need to be able to look at what life might be like for someone who is different to us.

Angelbooks' website provides an invaluable source of support and links for families, professionals and practitioners. Its refreshing, engaging approach enables us to develop as children and adults as we continue to discover the importance of 'me' and how we fit in our wonderful diverse world.

Visit: www.angelbooks.net | Email us: contactangelbooks@gmail.com